NORTH STAR

NORTH STAR

PHILLIPS KLOSS

Sunstone Press
Santa Fe, New Mexico

FIRST EDITION

Printed in the United States of America

Library of Congress Cataloging in Publication Data:

Kloss, Phillips Wray, 1902-
    North Star / Phillips Kloss.
            p.   cm
        ISBN 0-86534-182-6 (hardcover)   ISBN 978-1-63293-151-1 (softcover)
        I. Title.
PS3521/L65N6   1992
811'.52--dc20   91-45521
                                                CIP

Published in 1992 by Sunstone Press
            Post Office Box 2321
            Santa Fe, New Mexico 87501

CONTENTS

North Star

NORTH STAR

Watch the Big Dipper swing around the
        North Star with its pointer stars,
The whole earth swinging daily around the
            north and south polarizing of its
            axis as it swings yearly on its
            orbit around the sun,
And the whole solar universe swings
            on an unknown orbit conditioned by far
            greater universes such as Betelgeuse
            and Antares,
A multiverse of unimaginable magnitude,
            sphere within sphere, various frames
            of reference
Our own sphere containing animate existence,
            birds, animals, human endeavors, inventors
            builders, artists, composers, performers.
Sailors steered by the North Star, we all
            steer by a definite idea and
            definite purpose.

SUNSET PEAKS

Clouds above the sunset peaks
Blaze afire with smoke-like streaks
And colored music down below
Seems to flow alike aglow
Singing in the silver sage
Lifting the heart in rapturage.

POETIC TECHNIQUES

Rhythm gives force to sheer statement,
       rhyme secures it, iambic, anapest,
       paeonic, spondee, trimeter, tetrameter,
       hexameter, mixtures and deviations,
       Shelley the lushest binding and
       unbinding Prometheus "pinnacled
       dim in the intense inane."

MUSIC TECHNIQUES

Key signatures and time-figures are
      subject to the one-one beat of
      the heart, the drum, the metronome.
Arnold Schönberg probed deep
      with his conventional quartet
      writing, lost meaning with his
      twelve-tone-scale theory. Music
      is thought.

BEETHOVEN'S APASSIONATA
AND SIXTEENTH QUARTET

The power of the first movement of the
      Appassionata is immediate, the theme
      develops stronger and stronger, the final
      syncopation enhancing rather than
      shattering it, the ending on one
      note consolidating the climax, the
      piano the right instrument.
His sixteenth Quartet has a totally
      different construction, it is
      anguished, it is one of the world's
      great masterpieces, both pieces
      evocative of the Immortal Beloved.

BERLIOZ'S LACHRYMOSA

The exquisite descant of the high
      soprano over the thundering chorus
      of male and female voices wailing
      in ostentatious grief for the crucified
      Christ transcends tears.

HERMIT THRUSH

Go in the woods and hush and hush
Listen to the song of the hermit thrush
Ethereal voice of the solitude
Rebuking the noise of the multitude.

BREWER SPARROW

A drab little bird but his trill has
        the potentiality of all music in it,
        it fills you, thrills you, and he
        is the only bird who innovates a
        series of songs in flight or by his
        nest in his basaltic amphitheater.
        Innovates!

SNOWBIRDS

Hardly any song, juncos. grey-headed,
    black-headed, pink-sided, lovable
    little birds twittering together.
Some people shoot them for
    snowbird pie, an ugly way for
    them to die, ugly way for people
    to satisfy.

THE IRRECONCILABLE INTERNECINE

Cat mauling a mouse, goshawk clutching
      a quail, man slaughtering animals,
      man slaughtering man, tribe against tribe,
      nation against nation, religion against
      religion, ideology against ideology.
Jainists trample living things underfoot,
      vegetarians yank plants out of the ground,
      crush cook and eat them, eat eat eat, kill kill
      kill, breed breed breed, perpeturate the
      strife of life, the irreconcilable internecine.
'Tis a pitiless cosmos, existence consumed
      by existence, eon consumed by eon,
      to what end?
We cannot transcend, we can only confront,
      resolve, create.
Compassion is always with us for each other
      as we share the paradoxical pair good
      and evil, right and wrong, truth and beauty.

AMOEBA

Amoebas are the most elementary form of
     life. They reproduce by fission, a kind
     of structural conciousness.
Whatever evolvement we have had we
     articulate our fissions and fusions
     verbally.
Amoebas stay amoebic.

MEDUSA AND MEDEA

The names of Medusa and Medea alliterate
      and both were sorceresses.
Medusa had snaky locks and Medea stabbed
      her own children, very melodramatic.
The Carmel poet Robinson Jeffers elevated
      Medea above Euripedes but nobody
      rescued Medusa.

THE SNAKE CULT

Some Indians regard rattlesnakes as
      brothers, a taboo against killing them,
      they have the power to kill you.
It is not a Quetzalcoatl concept, rather
      an alliance, and absorption of power.
Our Garden of Eden origin myth,
      Adam and Eve tempted by a serpent
      to partake of forbidden fruit, yields
      to a Freudian interpretation.
The Minoan culture in Crete had a Snake
      Goddess at Gnossis, snakes writhing
      in her hands, lust writhing in her glands,
      fertility or not fertility.
The water moccassin, called cottonmouth, along
      the Mississippi side streams is a hideous
      snake when seen with its mouth open and
      fangs showing. Its bite is dangerous and it
      can bite under water.
The coral snake in southern states has a
      venom like a cobra's. It affects the nerves.
      You can't breathe. You suffocate to death.
In New Hampshire we put harmless little green
      snakes in our pockets, make pets of them.
A snake is a snake. To attribute metaphysical
      propensities to them
      is a verbal fantasy.

EINSTEIN AND FARADAY

Faraday's Cage anticipated Einstein's
  Relativity, two of the greatest
  thinkers, greatest men in the world
  history, generous and kind in
  their personal lives.
The frame of reference, the curvature of space
  amplified their gentility.

HEIFETZ

Performers, Jascha Heifetz the superlative
    violinist of all time, past present or
    future, incessant daily practice,
    self-criticism, self-discipline.
Nicolo Paganinni, dead in 1840, is
    not recorded for posterity.

EDISON

The electric bulb and phonograph,
      light and sound, one of our basic
      inventors, Thomas Alva Edison,
      the artistry and trashery he
      made possible, he himself
      with purity of soul.

LINCOLN

Rail splitter, fence builder, crop raiser,
       book reader, scholar, gaunt figure,
       gaunt mind, Abraham Lincoln's
       integrity set a precedent for his
       country, the Gettysburg speech
       written on his cuff, compassionate
       for all suffering, struggle, conflict.

KIT CARSON

Uneducated, illiterate Kit Carson had an
    inborn intelligence which friends like
    Captain Simpson helped him develop
    and communicate.
He was the pioneer scout for
    John C. Fremont's explorations.
He talked with Indian tribes by sign language.
    He fought the Navajo and Apache predators
    sweeping down from Athabasca, eventually
    helped them settle on reservations.
In the Civil Was he eluded the confederates
    surrounding General Kearney's forces,
    got the U.S. navy to save the situation.
    Appointed a general himself he led the
    victory at Glorieta Pass, the Gettysburg
    of the West, which marked the end of
    the Civil War.
He was a crack shot, soft-spoken, kind-hearted,
    likeable. He married Maria Josefa Jaramillo
    of Taos and is buried there.
Valour is the word that distinguishes him.

CHOICE

Whither the choice, thither the zest
One does one's best,
Ideas, ideals to think and feel,
Create, enjoy with utmost zeal.
Wander where we want to wander,
Ponder what we want to ponder,
Choices determine how far to go
In mysteries we can never know,
The North Star pivots the world around,
The multiverse is beyond beyondness.

ABOUT THE AUTHOR

Phillips Kloss was born in Webster Groves, Missouri in 1902.
His first aquaintance with New Mexico came in 1916 when
he worked on his brother's ranch. In 1925 he graduated from
the University of California at Berkeley. Two years later
he was back in New Mexico, this time with his wife,
Alice Geneva Glasier (Gene Kloss). In the years that followed,
living both in New Mexico and on the coast of California,
Mr. Kloss established himself nationally as an important poet
and critic. Today, Phillips and Gene Kloss live and work in
Taos, New Mexico. In addition to this volume, Sunstone Press has
published *The Great Kiva*, *Gene Kloss Etchings*, *Selected Poems of
Phillips Kloss*, *Rainbow Obsidian* and *The Taos Crescent*.